MATTESON PUBLIC LIBRARY
801 S. School Ave.
Matteson, IL 60443
Ph: 708-748-4431
www.mattesonpubliclibrary.org

Essential Issues

BINGE DRINKING

Essential Issues

Binge Drinking
BY STEPHANIE WATSON

Content Consultant
Stephen A. Lopez
College Assistant Professor, Health Science
New Mexico State University

ABDO
Publishing Company

Essential Issues

CREDITS

Published by ABDO Publishing Company, 8000 West 78th Street, Edina, Minnesota 55439. Copyright © 2012 by Abdo Consulting Group, Inc. International copyrights reserved in all countries. No part of this book may be reproduced in any form without written permission from the publisher. The Essential Library™ is a trademark and logo of ABDO Publishing Company.

Printed in the United States of America,
North Mankato, Minnesota
062011
092011

 THIS BOOK CONTAINS AT LEAST 10% RECYCLED MATERIALS.

Editor: Amy Van Zee
Copy Editor: Jennifer Joline Anderson
Cover Design: Marie Tupy
Interior Design and Production: Christa Schneider

Library of Congress Cataloging-in-Publication Data
Watson, Stephanie, 1969-
  Binge drinking / by Stephanie Watson.
    p. cm. -- (Essential issues)
  Includes bibliographical references.
  ISBN 978-1-61783-131-7
 1. Binge drinking--Juvenile literature. 2. Drinking of alcoholic beverages--Juvenile literature. 3. Youth--Alcohol use--Juvenile literature. 4. Binge drinking--United States--Juvenile literature. I. Title.
  HV5066.W38 2012
  362.292--dc22
                                            2011016734

Binge Drinking

TABLE OF CONTENTS

Chapter 1	A Life Lost	6
Chapter 2	The History of Binge Drinking	16
Chapter 3	Is Binge Drinking on the Rise?	26
Chapter 4	What Happens When People Binge Drink	34
Chapter 5	How Binge Drinking Affects Lives	42
Chapter 6	Binge Drinking and Young People	52
Chapter 7	Why Young People Drink	60
Chapter 8	Laws to Stop Binge Drinking	70
Chapter 9	Other Efforts to Prevent Binge Drinking	82

Timeline	96
Essential Facts	100
Glossary	102
Additional Resources	104
Source Notes	106
Index	109
About the Author	112

Binge drinking can lead to injuries, disease, and even death.

A Life Lost

Scott Eugene Roberts was a smart, nice kid. He had just finished his sophomore year at San Marcos High School in Carlsbad, California, where he was on both the junior varsity football and wrestling teams.

Binge Drinking

On Monday, June 22, 2009, Scott went to a friend's house in Carlsbad to celebrate the start of summer. He and his friends played a drinking game, and Scott consumed as many as 24 shots of liquor. The next morning, three of his friends found Scott lying on the floor surrounded by empty bottles of tequila, whiskey, and vodka. He was not breathing.

The friends tried to perform cardiopulmonary resuscitation (CPR), an emergency procedure, to get Scott's heart pumping and breathing started. But it was too late. When the police arrived, they pronounced Scott dead from alcohol poisoning. His blood alcohol content (BAC) was .39—nearly five times the amount at which a person is legally too drunk to drive. He was just 16 years old.

Scott was not an alcoholic. He liked to hang out with his friends and have a few drinks, but he did not realize that having too many alcoholic drinks at once could be deadly.

What Is Binge Drinking?

Binge drinking is the term for the type of drinking that killed Scott. Although binge drinking is not a new practice, the way scientists define it has changed over the years.

In 1992, Harvard University social psychologist Henry Wechsler launched an important study of college drinking. In the Public Health College Alcohol Study, Wechsler and his team of researchers conducted four different surveys of 50,000 students at 120 colleges in 40 states. The study spanned 14 years and helped researchers learn about the way young people drink.

Wechsler's study led to more than 80 journal articles and helped create a more exact definition for binge drinking. In 1994, Wechsler defined binge drinking as the act of consuming large enough amounts of alcohol in a short enough period of time to put the drinker, as well as other people, at risk. He came up with specific numbers to define binge drinking—five or more drinks for men, and four or more drinks for women, consumed in a short period of time, such as in one evening or one sitting. One standard drink equals 12 ounces (355 mL) of beer, 5 ounces (148 mL) of wine, or 1.5 ounces (44 mL) —a shot—of 80-proof liquor (such as gin, rum, vodka, or whiskey).

Wechsler was one of the first researchers to take into account the differences in how alcohol affects men and women. Women's bodies metabolize, or

Binge Drinking

break down, alcohol differently than men's bodies do. This is why women feel the effects of drinking more quickly than men. For this reason, Wechsler found that a lower number of drinks could be dangerous for women.

Research has found that men who have five or more drinks in one sitting and women who have four or more drinks in one sitting at least once during a two-week period are much more likely to get into fights, drive while drunk, get into trouble with the law, and vandalize property. People who are around binge drinkers may also be at risk. For example, the drinker might punch and injure someone during a fight or run over a pedestrian while driving drunk.

Many of the biggest health organizations agree with Wechsler's definition of binge drinking. The US surgeon general, the US Centers

Alcohol Content in Different Drinks

When vodka is 80 proof, or a bottle of beer reads "4.6 percent alcohol," what do those numbers mean? Proof and alcohol percent measure the amount of alcohol in a beverage in proportion to the total liquid volume.

The percent of alcohol in a beverage is measured using a hydrometer—an instrument that measures density, or mass per volume. Because alcohol has a lower density than water, as the amount of alcohol in a beverage increases, the density decreases.

The "proof" equals the percentage of alcohol in that beverage, times two. So a mixture that is 45 percent alcohol would be 90 proof. Brewers express the amount of alcohol in their beers as a percentage. Usually beers contain between 3 and 5 percent alcohol by volume.

for Disease Control and Prevention (CDC), and the National Institute on Drug Abuse all use the five/four drink measure to define binge drinking. When other researchers study binge drinking, they also use the five/four drink measure. Using the same numbers to define binge drinking makes studies consistent.

Issues with the Five/Four Drink Definition

Wechsler spent many years researching binge drinking before coming up with his definition, and many health organizations agree with his numbers. However, some experts say it is not a very accurate way

---

What Is BAC?

Blood alcohol content or blood alcohol concentration (BAC) is the concentration of alcohol in someone's blood. It is measured as a percentage of the person's blood. For example, a BAC of 0.1 percent means that one-tenth of a percent of the person's blood is alcohol.

A person's BAC is based on how much he or she drinks. It also has to do with the person's size, metabolism, how much he or she eats while drinking, how quickly the drinks are consumed, and how strong the drinks are. A small person who drinks vodka all night without eating anything will have a higher BAC than a large person who drinks beer along with a big meal.

Someone with a BAC of .08 or higher is considered legally drunk—too drunk to drive. Many factors affect how a person metabolizes alcohol, but estimates show how much alcohol would bring a person to the illegal limit. For example, a 130-pound (59-kg) woman who consumed three drinks over a period of two hours on an empty stomach would have a BAC of approximately .086, depending on her metabolism.

Binge Drinking

to define binge drinking. One argument is that five drinks for men and four for women are not enough drinks to be considered binge drinking. According to the CDC, the average binge drinker actually consumes eight alcoholic drinks in a two-hour period.

Wechsler's definition does not take into account how many hours it takes someone to finish the drinks. It also does not consider how much the person weighs, how much alcohol is in each drink, or whether the person eats food while drinking. However, all of these factors determine how alcohol affects the body and brain and whether someone will get drunk from the amount of alcohol he or she consumes.

Wechsler's measure of binge drinking also does not consider whether a person is drunk. Someone who has five drinks over an entire evening while having dinner with friends might not feel strong effects from the alcohol. On the other hand, a very thin person who does not eat anything while drinking might start exhibiting signs of impairment after just one or two drinks. Some health organizations get around that problem by defining binge drinking based on the BAC. The National

Institute on Alcohol Abuse and Alcoholism (NIAAA) considers someone a binge drinker when he or she develops a pattern of drinking enough to raise the BAC to .08 or higher in one episode. That is the illegal intoxication limit in most states.

Other groups argue that the term *binge drinking* should not be used at all. The Inter-Association Task Force on Alcohol and Other Substance Abuse Issues, a group of educators who work to prevent substance abuse, reject Wechsler's definition of binge drinking. They claim it is too vague because it does not consider the drinker's size or other factors that impact whether a person gets drunk. They recommend using terms such as *high risk*, *harmful use*, and *blood alcohol concentration* instead.

Experts might not agree on a definition for binge drinking. However, they do agree that consuming several drinks in just a few hours can be dangerous. Binge drinking does not only impact the health and safety of the person who

Binge Drinking Deaths

Scott Eugene Roberts is just one of many teens who have lost their lives to binge drinking in recent years. In September 2004, 19-year-old Samantha Spady was found dead in a Colorado State University fraternity house. She had finished 30 to 40 beers and vodka drinks in just a few hours. Soon after that, freshman Lynn Gordon Bailey Jr. died after having too many drinks at a fraternity at a different Colorado school. He was 18 years old. Many other high school and college students have also died after binge drinking episodes.

Binge Drinking

Approximately 800 people gathered at the memorial for student Samantha Spady, who died after binge drinking in 2004.

is drinking. It can involve everyone around that person, including entire communities.

Binge drinking is not a new problem. People have been using alcohol in rituals, as medicine, as a beverage, and for their enjoyment for thousands of years. Yet it was only in the mid- to late-twentieth century that researchers and public health officials began realizing how dangerous this type of drinking might be, and the first efforts were made to curb binge drinking.

Essential Issues

"Alcohol remains the most heavily abused substance by America's youth. We can no longer ignore what alcohol is doing to our children. . . . Underage drinking is everybody's problem—and its solution is everyone's responsibility."[1]
—*Former acting surgeon general Kenneth P. Moritsugu*

As the understanding of binge drinking and its effects has grown, these efforts have expanded to involve schools, doctors, community and nonprofit organizations, and government programs. Young adults aged 15–24 are the group most at risk. When people under age 21 drink alcohol, approximately 90 percent of the time they are binge drinking. For that reason, many of the binge drinking prevention efforts today focus on high school and college students.

Binge Drinking

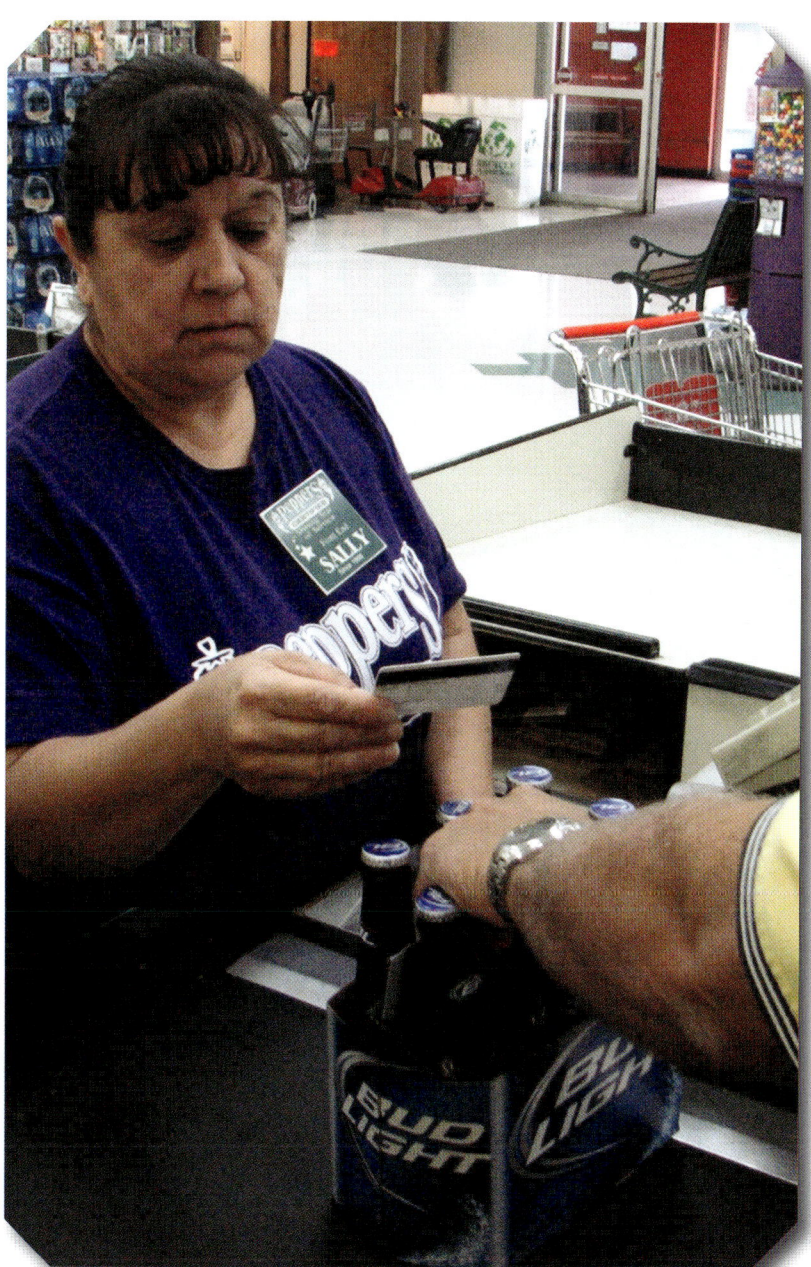

Supermarket clerk Sally Montaño checks identification for an alcohol purchase. Binge drinking is especially common among underage drinkers.

Chapter 2

A woodcut depicts alcohol use in Europe in the sixteenth century.

The History of Binge Drinking

Alcohol has been around for tens of thousands of years. The first alcoholic drinks were probably discovered by accident. When yeast—a single-celled fungus—makes its way into fruit or grains, it eats up the sugar and turns it into

Binge Drinking

alcohol. This process is called fermentation. People may have become intoxicated while eating fermented fruits or grain. Eventually, people learned how to ferment drinks themselves from berries, grapes, grains, and honey.

Besides making those who drink it feel giddy, in its early days, alcohol served several useful purposes. Beer and wine were important sources of nutrition. Alcohol was loaded with the protein, fat, vitamins, and carbohydrates that were lacking in the meager diets people ate many years ago. Alcohol was also considered good medicine. The Sumerian civilization, which thrived around 2000 BCE in what is now Iraq, used the beer and wine they produced as medical treatments. Nursing mothers were told to drink beer to increase lactation. Even in the modern age, some doctors instruct their patients to drink moderate amounts of alcohol to improve their health.

In ancient times as today, beer and wine were used in social and religious rituals. People drank to celebrate a child's birth, a marriage, a death, and various festivals. Both the Egyptians and the Babylonians offered beer and wine to their gods and goddesses. When Egyptians died, beer was often

Essential Issues

Beer for Breakfast?

During the time of the Tudors, who ruled England from 1485 to 1603, beer was such a popular drink that it was served as freely as people drink water today. Beer was healthier than the polluted water of the time, so the English enjoyed it with every meal—even breakfast. A typical breakfast for an earl and his countess at the time might have consisted of two loaves of bread, some salt fish and herring, and a quart (.9 L) each of beer and wine. Mary, Queen of Scots, reportedly enjoyed ale with her beef each morning.

placed in their tombs so they could take it with them to the afterlife.

Finally, alcohol was an important thirst quencher. By the Middle Ages, many of the rivers and streams in Europe had turned into sewers. They were horribly polluted from all the waste thrown into them by neighboring cities and towns. The water smelled horrible, tasted even worse, and was often so full of bacteria that it was deadly to drink. Because alcohol goes through a process of filtering and boiling, beer was considered a much healthier alternative to potentially polluted drinking water. Additionally, alcoholic beverages such as beer, wine, and ale provided sailors with a safe drink when they were on long voyages. For all of these reasons, people began drinking in earnest.

Early Warnings

Even thousands of years ago, there were people who drank too much.

Binge Drinking

Any laws about drinking that did exist at the time did not punish the drinkers. Instead, they punished the people who served the alcohol.

After the Middle Ages, people began moving from rural areas into cities. Trade grew, and with it, prosperity increased. People drank alcohol socially and to avoid polluted water. By the sixteenth century, people were drinking a lot. In Coventry, England, the average person drank 17 pints of beer and ale each week. An English sailor was rationed a gallon (3.8 L) of beer each day. People also had more types of alcohol from

The Gin Epidemic

During the Middle Ages, most people in England drank beer and ale. Gin was invented in the seventeenth century, but only a small number of British companies were allowed to operate distilleries. Therefore, gin and other distilled drinks were too expensive for most English people to afford.

That changed in 1689, when the British Parliament opened up distillation in order to use up surplus grain and raise tax revenues. Gin prices dropped until gin became even less expensive than beer. Poor people who had never been able to afford hard liquor before began drinking it in large amounts. This led to what was called the Gin Epidemic, a period in which gin drinking exploded in England. In 1700, people in England and Wales drank about 1.23 million gallons (4.66 million L) of gin a year. By 1751, they were drinking more than 7 million gallons (26.5 million L) a year.

The British government realized it needed to do something to stop the Gin Epidemic. Parliament passed the Tippling Act of 1751, which imposed regulations on gin sales. Smaller gin shops closed, gin prices rose, and gin drinking dropped in England.

which to choose. Not only did wine and beer flow freely, but the introduction of a heating process called distillation led to the production of whiskey, gin, and other types of alcoholic drinks. At the time, drinking was still viewed as normal, and even healthy. By the eighteenth century, that view would start to change.

One reason for the change in attitude about alcohol was religion. Wine has long been part of many religious rituals. Jews drink wine from a Kiddush cup on the Sabbath. Christians drink wine to represent the blood of Christ. Yet Christian and Jewish teachings emphasize moderation. Some religions prescribe abstinence from alcohol altogether, considering it morally wrong.

Not only was drinking to excess seen as immoral, but it also was bad for business. With the Industrial Revolution of the eighteenth century came a need for focused, efficient labor. People who were drunk or hungover did not make good workers. In addition to slowing down production, alcohol took the blame for many of society's problems at the time. Crime, poverty, infant deaths—drinking was supposedly behind all of them. Religious groups and other concerned individuals began calling for temperance,

A temperance pledge circa 1900

or moderation. The temperance movement began gaining momentum in the early nineteenth century and continued on. Eventually, there would be a call in the United States for prohibition—a complete halt to all alcohol use. It would eventually climax with the Prohibition Era, which made the distribution of alcohol illegal in the United States from 1920 to 1933.

Even though religion and society frowned upon drinking to excess, people kept doing it. Those who drank too much were seen as fools who could not control their behavior. Instead of getting help, they were ridiculed or sent to prison. However, the way society viewed binge drinking began changing in the middle of the twentieth century.

New Attitudes about Drinking

In 1945, a movie called *The Lost Weekend* was released into theaters. It tells the story of an alcoholic named Don Birnam who went on a four-day bender. *Bender* is a word people use to describe binge drinking. At the time, binge drinking was considered to be a period of drinking that went on for several days. Usually, a person who went on a binge or a bender was an alcoholic, like Birnam.

The Lost Weekend exposed the perils of too much drinking. In one scene, Birnam fell down a flight of stairs and knocked himself unconscious. Before

Binge Drinking

The Lost Weekend, Hollywood had made light of alcoholism, portraying alcoholics as silly, staggering drunks. For the first time, this movie prompted audiences to recognize the serious health problems and dangers alcohol can cause.

Around the time *The Lost Weekend* was made, the definition of binge drinking also began changing. This change had a lot to do with the work of E. Morton Jellinek, a researcher at Yale University who began studying problem drinking in the 1930s. Jellinek found that alcoholism was not a sign of moral weakness or a lack of willpower, as people thought at the time. In 1952, he argued that alcoholism was a disease of dependence that could cause serious health problems and needed to be treated.

Jellinek's work led to more research on alcohol use. Researchers learned that some groups of people,

Alcohol as Medicine

Throughout the ages, many doctors have recommended alcohol for its vitamin and mineral content. Hippocrates, a Greek physician who lived from 460 to 377 BCE, recommended wine as a treatment for nearly every ailment. During the American Civil War (1861–1865), beer was called "liquid bread" because it contained so many important nutrients that soldiers were lacking in their diets.

Doctors continue to recognize that the moderate consumption of alcohol can have positive health benefits. Research has found that a glass or two of red wine each day might help prevent heart disease and diabetes. Yet doctors also emphasize that binge or heavy drinking can lead to cancer, high blood pressure, and heart damage. Some doctors are hesitant to encourage a patient to begin drinking alcohol for its benefits, some of which might be found in other nonalcoholic sources.

especially college students, were not going on benders that lasted for many days. Instead, they were drinking numerous alcoholic beverages in the same day as a way to socialize. Researchers continued studying the habits of those who used alcohol.

By the 1990s, the definition of binge drinking had changed. The term is now used to describe a single period of time during which a person consumes enough alcoholic drinks to get drunk. Often the binge drinker is a teenager or a young adult. In 1994, Wechsler finally put an exact number on the amount of drinks considered a binge—five for men, and four for women.

Binge Drinking

Actor Ray Milland in a scene from The Lost Weekend

Chapter 3

Students gather at a pub in Massachusetts in 2002.

Is Binge Drinking on the Rise?

On any Friday or Saturday night, bars and private parties—often on college campuses—are packed with young people who are there to have a good time. Often, having a good time means that students down drink after drink until they are buzzed or drunk. It would seem from looking in these bars and parties that a lot of young people are binge drinking. But are more teens really binge drinking today than in years past, or are binge drinking episodes just being reported more often?

Who Is Binge Drinking?

Approximately 15 percent of Americans admit to binge drinking. From the news reports, it might seem as though students are doing most of the binge drinking. It is true that alcohol use is a problem among high school and college students. When young people drink, they tend to do it in binges, often with the goal of getting drunk.

Some kids try their first alcoholic drink as young as age nine or ten. By age 13, almost one-third of kids have started drinking. At age 15, half of kids have started drinking. And by age 21, almost everyone has at least tried alcohol. In high school, many kids drink large quantities of alcohol on a

How Does the Legal Drinking Age Affect Binge Drinking?

Some experts say one of the reasons young people binge drink is because drinking is forbidden. According to this idea, kids get a thrill out of disobeying their parents—and the drinking age laws.

By this reasoning, it would make sense that countries with a lower drinking age would have less of a problem with binge drinking. Yet this does not seem to be true. In Great Britain, where the drinking age is 18, more than half of teenagers report binge drinking. Denmark, which also has a drinking age of 18, has a serious problem with teen binge drinking—the highest rate in all of Europe.

regular basis. Approximately 42 percent of high school students say they drink, and one in four binge drink. The rate of binge drinking episodes is highest among young adults of college age—those aged 18 to 25. At college, they find it easier to drink without getting into trouble—even if they are still underage. College students spend approximately $5.5 billion each year on alcohol, which is more than they spend on soft drinks or their college textbooks. Binge drinking is more common among college athletes, fraternity members, and sorority members.

> **Peer Pressure to Drink**
>
> Peer pressure can be a powerful influence on youth. It can be very hard for high school—and even college—students to "just say no" when everybody else is drinking. Pressure from their friends and classmates can lead students to try a lot of things they would not have tried otherwise, including drinking, smoking cigarettes, and taking drugs.
>
> Binge drinking is just one of the many unhealthy activities that are strongly influenced by peer pressure. In high school, kids binge drink to fit in. In college, drinking is seen as expected—the normal thing to do.
>
> This is especially true in social fraternities and sororities. Despite numerous laws and policies prohibiting it, pledging into a frat or sorority house often involves hazing—a process in which new pledges are pressured into taking part in an initiation rite. Often that initiation involves alcohol—and in large amounts. Fraternity and sorority houses regularly have parties in which they serve alcohol, and it is often served to students who are underage. In one study by the Harvard School of Public Health, 75 percent of frat members reported that they were heavy drinkers. By comparison, 49 percent of students who were not frat members said they were heavy drinkers.

Binge Drinking

Youth ages 12 to 20 who drink consume an average of five drinks each occasion, which is considered binge drinking. By comparison, adults who drink usually have approximately two or three drinks at a time. Nearly half of all full-time college students say they binge drink at least once a month, and when they do drink, they almost always do it to get drunk. A report by Wechsler and Toben F. Nelson noted that almost 30 percent of students say they get drunk three or more times a month. By comparison, the Alcohol Drug Abuse Resource Center reported that approximately 35 percent of 26–34 year olds and approximately 19 percent of those older than 35 reported binge drinking in 2007. Although some adults who binge drink are already heavy drinkers, people who do not usually drink a lot account for almost half of all binge-drinking episodes. It may be that these occasional drinkers go overboard while celebrating a special occasion, such as a birthday or a high school reunion. It may also be that some have difficulty controlling their intake once they begin drinking.

Binge drinking is more common among men than women. Results from a CDC study showed that binge drinking was twice as common among male

Essential Issues

Madison, Wisconsin, a college town, limits the number of new bars to help combat binge drinking.

respondents than female respondents. Also, among adults, binge drinking is more common among people who have money—those who earn more than

$75,000 a year. People who have money can more easily afford to spend it on alcohol.

Binge Drinking—
The Real Numbers

Even though statistics about binge drinking are available, it is hard for researchers to know exactly how many people binge drink. Sometimes, people are embarrassed to tell researchers how much they really drink. This makes researchers wonder if numbers are actually higher than tests and surveys show.

It might seem as though binge drinking is on the rise. Stories about teens who drank too much and got into trouble can be found all over news shows and Internet sites. Although it is true that binge drinking is a common problem, the numbers are not increasing as much as people might think—in fact, some sources report that incidents of binge

How Much Are Binge Drinkers Really Drinking?

Studies find that a very small percentage of drinkers are responsible for most of the alcohol that is consumed in the United States. Binge drinkers make up less than a quarter of the US population. However, they drink more than three-quarters of all the alcohol consumed, according to the US Department of Justice. People who are frequent bingers—those who binge drink often—make up only 7 percent of the population, yet they drink 45 percent of all the alcohol.

drinking among high school students might be decreasing. However, the percentage of students who binge drink on college campuses has stayed steady over the years at approximately 40 percent.

How Geography Affects Drinking

Where a person lives might have a big effect on whether he or she binge drinks. Every year, America's Health Rankings, a group that tracks US health trends, ranks states by different health measures, including high blood pressure, obesity, and alcohol use.

This health survey also ranks states by the number of binge drinkers as a percentage of the state's total population. In 2010, the states with the highest percentage of binge drinkers were Wisconsin (23.2 percent), North Dakota (21.5 percent), and Minnesota (20 percent). Utah (8.6 percent) and Tennessee (8.8 percent) had the lowest percentage of binge drinkers, followed by West Virginia (9 percent).

Binge Drinking

Members of a New Jersey youth alliance placed stickers on alcoholic beverages to remind customers not to distribute alcohol to underage teens.

Chapter 4

After binge drinking, a person may experience a headache and other hangover symptoms.

What Happens When People Binge Drink

No matter who is doing it, binge drinking is not without consequences. Alcohol can have a profound effect on the body, especially when large amounts are consumed over a short period of time. Alcohol makes its way to the stomach and intestines, where it is absorbed and then sent flowing into the bloodstream. Through the blood, alcohol can travel freely to all of the body's tissues, including the brain.

Binge Drinking and the Body

The body treats alcohol as a toxin. It is the liver's job to metabolize alcohol so it can be removed from the body. However, the liver can only break down a little bit of alcohol at a time—approximately one drink each hour. Drinking more than that amount can be too much for the liver to handle. The extra alcohol builds up in the blood, causing the BAC to rise.

The more drinks a person consumes, the greater the effects on his or her body. Other factors that also determine the effects of alcohol include a person's size, weight, age, and sex. Also important is how quickly and how much the person drinks, and how much food is eaten while

Binge Drinking versus Alcoholism

A binge drinker is not the same as an alcoholic. Alcoholics drink heavily on a regular basis, and when they stop drinking, their body craves more alcohol. Binge drinkers do not necessarily have the same physical or emotional cravings that alcoholics feel.

However, frequent binge drinking is referred to as *episodic alcoholism* or *dipsomania*. These terms apply to those who exhibit signs that binge drinking is affecting their lives in significant ways. For teens, this often includes violent outbursts, fights, difficulty with school, parental conflicts, and health problems.

drinking. Eating while drinking or having food already in the stomach can lessen the effects of alcohol.

Young people are more sensitive to the effects of alcohol than adults, yet they may not be aware of as many of the negative effects, such as a hangover. For example, a college student may go out to a party with her friends. She has a couple of beers. The drinks make her more talkative. She laughs and chats with her friends, saying things she was much too shy or embarrassed to say before she started drinking. Though this student seems to be having a great time, with each drink her body is becoming more affected.

This student has two more beers, then another one. Now she is feeling a lot less happy. As the alcohol affects her brain and nervous system, the room starts to spin. She feels tired and her speech sounds slurred. The alcohol irritates her stomach, making her feel nauseated. One drink more, and she has to run to the bathroom to throw up. Her friends call a cab, because she is much too drunk to drive a car.

The next morning, this college student wakes up feeling like someone hit her in the head and stomach with a hammer. Her head is throbbing. She feels sick to her stomach. She is so tired she can barely get out of bed. She has a hangover.

Binge Drinking

This story illustrates that alcohol is a kind of poison. When it gets into the system, the bloodstream carries it to just about every organ. Alcohol decreases breathing and heart rates, strains the kidneys, and causes dehydration. These are examples of acute, or sudden and short-term, effects of alcohol on the body.

Chronic, or long-term, effects of alcohol abuse include inflammation and cancer of the liver, lungs, or throat. Additionally, long-term abuse of alcohol can lead to an irreversible liver disease called cirrhosis. Symptoms of cirrhosis include nausea, vomiting, impotence in men, weakness, and weight loss.

Alcohol Poisoning

Alcohol poisoning is a very serious condition brought on by drinking too much alcohol. Every year, thousands of people go to hospital emergency rooms for alcohol poisoning. Some, such as Winona State University student Jenna Foellmi, die from it. On December 13, 2007, Foellmi drank for most of the day and evening and then passed out. The next morning, her body was cold. The medical examiner declared her dead of acute alcohol poisoning.

People who get alcohol poisoning may show various signs. They can become very confused. Their breathing slows, and their body temperature drops. Their skin may appear pale or even blue. Some people with alcohol poisoning have seizures—fits caused by problems with the brain's electric activity. A person with alcohol poisoning can go into a coma. Others might believe the person is sleeping or passed out, but a coma is much more dangerous. The person can become brain damaged or even die. That is why it is important to call 911 if someone has had too much alcohol and is showing any of these signs.

Essential Issues

Some cirrhosis patients require a liver transplant, and some die from the disease as toxins build up in their system and cause their organs to shut down.

Alcohol on the Brain

The brain controls breathing, heartbeat, temperature, appetite, movement, and just about every other important body function. When someone drinks heavily, alcohol reaches the brain and slows down its activity. People who are drunk cannot react as quickly as usual. For example, if a drunk man is driving a car and someone runs out in front of him, it takes extra time for his brain to send a message to his foot that he needs to step on the brake. Alcohol can also affect perception and judgment to the point that the driver may not realize he needs to step on the brake.

Oftentimes, people who have been drinking slur their speech and

A Life Lost to Alcohol Poisoning

In the fall of 1997, 18-year-old Scott Krueger was beginning his freshman year at the Massachusetts Institute of Technology (MIT). He decided to pledge a fraternity—Phi Gamma Delta.

During the pledge celebration, older frat members left Krueger and the other new pledges in a room filled with alcohol. They challenged the pledges to finish all the alcohol in the room.

Krueger drank about 15 shots of alcohol in an hour. Then he started complaining that he was not feeling well. His frat brothers carried him upstairs and laid him on a bed. About ten minutes later, frat members could not wake up Krueger. They called the police. By the time an ambulance arrived, Krueger had turned blue. He was rushed to the hospital. He remained in a coma until three days later, when he was pronounced dead from alcohol poisoning.

Binge Drinking

Alcohol slows the brain's reaction times. Those who drive while intoxicated cannot operate their cars properly.

stumble when they try to walk. When police pull over drunk drivers, they ask these drivers to walk a straight line and stand on one leg for 30 seconds. These tasks are easy for someone who is sober, but people who are drunk have a harder time coordinating their body movements because alcohol has affected their brains.

These are examples of short-term impairments, but binge drinking over and over again can have long-term effects on the brain. Binge drinking can affect attention, concentration, and memory.

Essential Issues

A Serious Brain Disease

Many people who abuse alcohol get sick. One very serious brain disease that affects people who drink heavily is called Wernicke-Korsakoff syndrome. It is caused by a lack of vitamin B1 (thiamine). Many alcoholics do not get enough of this vitamin because they do not eat a healthy, balanced diet.

Wernicke-Korsakoff syndrome is really two diseases in one. One of the two diseases (Wernicke) causes confusion. People who have this disease are unable to walk normally, and their eyes make strange movements. The other disease (Korsakoff) causes learning and memory problems. The two diseases combined are very serious—even life threatening.

Heavy drinkers can also experience personality or mood changes, such as feeling more anxious or sad than usual.

Alcohol slowly damages the brain, both directly and because it affects the body's overall health. It can stop the brain from making new nerve cells, called neurons. These cells carry messages in the brain. A loss of neurons can affect a person's memory and ability to learn. Over time, the brain can actually shrink. These effects on the brain can continue even after someone stops drinking.

Binge Drinking

In some schools, law enforcement officers visit classrooms and bring special goggles that impair vision to simulate the effects of alcohol.

Chapter 5

An Alabama bar installed a Breathalyzer to help drinkers determine if they are too drunk to drive.

How Binge Drinking Affects Lives

While alcohol is harming the body, it is also harming other areas of a person's life, including work, school, and relationships. When people binge drink they do things they might not do sober, such as fighting or trying dangerous

Binge Drinking

stunts. They have trouble staying in school or keeping a steady job because they are too hungover and tired to work. People who drive after they have been drinking can get arrested. They might even hurt or kill someone on the road—maybe someone they love.

Drinking too much at once can lead to blackouts. During these episodes, people cannot remember details of what they did. They might forget an entire night. Many of those who experienced blackouts later found out they had taken part in dangerous activities, such as vandalism, drunk driving, or unprotected sex.

Bad Decisions

Drinking affects judgment, which is the process used to determine whether an action is smart or stupid. Poor judgment leads people to act differently drunk than sober. Teens

Blackouts

Blackouts occur when the BAC rises very quickly. Although the person can walk and talk, he or she will not remember anything. Alcohol prevents the brain from forming new memories. Every event that happens while someone is having a blackout disappears from the mind, almost as though it never happened. Someone who has a blackout might not remember doing something dangerous, such as stealing a car or having unprotected sex. Having blackouts is a clear sign that someone is drinking too much.

Essential Issues

are already very impulsive because they are still growing and maturing. When they are drunk, they can make really bad decisions that put their health—and lives—at serious risk. One of those bad decisions is to have sex with someone they do not know, or to have sex without using protection. Having unprotected sex can lead to an unplanned pregnancy, or a deadly disease such as acquired immunodeficiency syndrome (AIDS). Poor judgment is why underage drinking contributes to the three biggest causes of death in people ages 12 to 20—unintentional injury, homicide, and suicide.

Pulled Over by Police

What happens when a police officer pulls over a drunk driver? When a police officer sees a car weaving back and forth across the road, he or she signals for the driver to pull over. The officer talks to the driver, and if the officer suspects that the driver is drunk, he or she needs to do a series of tests to prove it.

The driver will have to take a field sobriety test. The officer will ask him or her to walk a straight line, stand on one leg, and follow a moving object with the eyes. If the driver fails these tests, the officer may use a Breathalyzer test to check the driver's BAC.

A Breathalyzer is a machine that measures the BAC in the breath. As blood flows through the lungs, some of the alcohol from the blood moves into the air sacs, or alveoli. As the air from the alveoli is breathed out, alcohol can be detected in each breath. When the driver blows into a tube attached to the Breathalyzer, the machine measures the amount of alcohol in that breath. Drivers whose BAC is .08 or above can be arrested for drunk driving and have their driver's licenses taken away.

Binge Drinking

Minnesota law enforcement officer Matthew Owens giving a field sobriety test

DRINKING AND DRIVING

One of the worst judgment calls binge drinkers make is to get behind the wheel of a car while drunk.

Binge drinkers are 14 times more likely to drive while under the influence than people who do not binge drink. In one study, approximately 12 percent of binge drinkers said they drove during or within two hours of a binge-drinking episode. About a quarter of these drivers said they had consumed ten or more drinks before driving.

Alcohol makes it much harder to pay attention to the road. It slows judgment, which means that it can take longer to turn the wheel. A person whose BAC is well below the .08 illegal limit can be impaired enough to cause a crash.

Police pull over drivers they suspect of being drunk. People who are caught driving drunk can lose their driver's license, face high fines, and even go to jail. Legal consequences for underage drinkers are different. In many states, the illegal limit while driving is .02 for those under age 21. Even if the driver's BAC is under this limit, in many states the driver may be charged with the crime of underage drinking.

Violence

Alcohol is a powerful substance. Drinking can make it more likely for a person to make a bad decision

Binge Drinking

and can bring out violence. That is why people are more likely to hurt themselves and others while under the influence.

Rape is another very serious form of violence. Even if two people are dating, if one person says no and the other does not stop, it is considered rape. A person who has been drinking heavily might not have the judgment to realize that no means no. The person can go to jail as a result. Every year, almost 100,000 students are victims of sexual assault or date rape with alcohol involved.

Injuries

When people drink heavily, they may mistakenly believe they can do anything. They are more likely to try dangerous stunts, such as climbing out of a third-story window and walking across a ledge, or jumping off a steep hill. The alcohol makes them far less coordinated than they

Dangerous Accidents

In 1998, Leslie Baltz was an honors student at the University of Virginia. In December of that year, the college senior and her friends were drinking to celebrate the last home football game of the season. She got so drunk that she passed out on a couch in her friend's apartment. Her friends left her there to sleep off the alcohol while they went to the football game.

When her friends got back that night, they found Baltz unconscious on the floor after having fallen down the stairs. Her friends called 911, and Baltz was rushed to the hospital, where she was pronounced dead from brain injuries caused by her fall. She was 21 years old.

In 2007, Ohio high school students witnessed a mock crash meant to show possible consequences of drinking and driving.

were when they were sober. This can lead to serious accidents.

Drinking can contribute to all kinds of injuries, including falls, drownings, burns, and gun accidents. Some of these accidents are minor. One study found that people who drink are four times more likely than nondrinkers to fall and get other injuries. Binge drinkers are at even greater risk for injury. "Binge drinking is associated with over half of the 79,000 alcohol-attributable deaths in the United States each year," said Dr. Robert Brewer, alcohol program leader for the National Center for Chronic Disease Prevention and Health Promotion at the CDC.[1]

Alcohol's Other Big Risks

Vandalism is another big problem linked to drinking. Approximately 11 percent of college students say they have damaged property while drinking. And binge drinking can also put a student's education at risk. Students who binge drink are more likely to show up late or miss classes, forget to do their homework, and

Alcohol and Drowning

Because alcohol impairs judgment and affects the way the body functions, it is often a contributing factor in water-related accidents and deaths. The CDC reports that alcohol is related to one in five boating deaths and as many as half of all deaths associated with water recreation.

According to Dr. Robert D. Foss, a research scientist at the University of North Carolina, "It's not just crashing into other boats or piers that is causing the deaths. Frequently, people who have been drinking fall in the water even if a boat is not moving, become disoriented and drown."[2]

neglect to study for tests. Their grades can drop, and they might even be kicked out of school.

Some people who binge drink develop a problem with alcohol. They need or depend on drinking just to get through their day. Dependence can turn to alcoholism—a serious problem that can affect a person's health, friendships, and future.

Binge Drinking

While intoxicated, drunk youths uprooted and destroyed crosses in a World War I cemetery in France in 2010.

Chapter 6

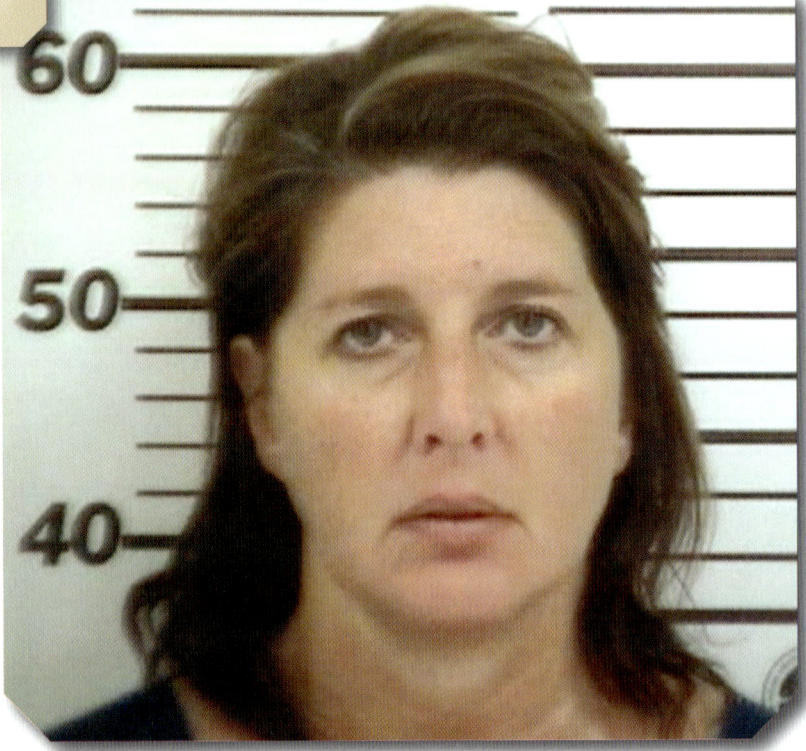

In 2009, Karen Downs faced charges for serving alcohol to teens at her daughter's fourteenth birthday party. Two teens were hospitalized.

Binge Drinking and Young People

The consequences of binge drinking can be serious and long lasting, but some effects of binge drinking are especially painful for young people. Plans for the future can be crushed by the negative consequences of binge drinking. Even though teens are not old enough to drink legally in the United States, many binge drink anyway. In a body that is still growing, the effects of too much alcohol are even more severe than they are in an adult.

Drinking not only can affect a young person's health, it can also affect his or her mind. Even though the rest of the body might have stopped growing, the brain continues to develop until around age 24. A teen's brain is more sensitive to the effects of alcohol than an adult's brain. That is why teens who drink score lower on vocabulary tests, have more trouble remembering, and perform worse in school than their friends who do not drink. According to Dr. Aaron White of Duke University,

> It has become clear that, during adolescence . . . the brain is highly plastic and shaped by experience. . . . Alcohol appears to interfere with the changes in circuitry that occur during learning.[1]

Alcohol, Drugs, and Intellectual Tests

A 2010 study by researchers at the University of New Mexico showed that teens who abuse alcohol and drugs scored more poorly on intellectual tests than teens who abstain. The tests measured attention, memory, verbal reasoning, visual perception, and other abilities. For those who continued drinking, the study showed that their test scores lowered after a year. Robert J. Thoma, the lead author of the study, said, "The most important thing in kids' lives is school. If you have a problem with sustained attention, then how are you going to do in math class? These kids are making things more difficult for themselves."[2]

Alcohol can make kids sad because it acts like a depressant on the brain. According to the Third National Health and Nutrition Survey, teenage girls who drink are four times more likely to be depressed than their peers who do not drink.

Drinking too much can also lead to weight gain, because alcohol is packed with calories. A single bottle of beer can contain 150 calories, which means that drinking five beers in a night adds up to about 750 calories—about the same as the calories found in a greasy fast-food burger. Excessive drinking can make teens overweight, leading to health problems such as high blood pressure, heart disease, and diabetes.

Long-Term Damage

Over time, alcohol can permanently damage the cells and tissues of the body. It can damage the liver cells that break down alcohol, leading to cirrhosis. Alcohol can also cause the pancreas to swell up.

Athletes and Alcohol

Binge drinking can have a big impact on a student's performance in school. Drinking too much can also affect a student's performance on the field, court, and track.

Alcohol slows reaction time and reduces hand-eye coordination, making it much harder to catch a game-winning pass. It also weakens the heart's pumping power. When the heart does not pump effectively, it cannot send as much blood to the body. Less blood means less oxygen to help the muscles work effectively. Weak muscles cannot run or jump as far.

Alcohol can also dehydrate the body. It is hard to perform well athletically without enough water. Dehydration can be very dangerous. It can even lead to seizures, a coma, or death.

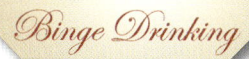
Binge Drinking

People who binge drink are more likely to get heart disease or have a heart attack or a stroke. Drinking increases the risk for just about every kind of cancer, including cancers of the mouth, voice box, liver, and esophagus.

Alcohol Abuse and Alcoholism

For some people, drinking is not just a way to spend time with friends—it is a habit they cannot shake. Alcohol is an addictive substance. Over time, a person can start to need it just to get through the day. Alcohol becomes a craving that does not go away. When an alcoholic tries to stop drinking, he or she can have a physical response that includes tremors, hallucinations, and shaking.

The younger someone is when he or she starts drinking, the more difficult it is to stop. Kids who start drinking before age 15 are five times more likely to become dependent on alcohol than adults who begin drinking at age 21 or older.

Binge Drinking, Spring Break, and Prom

Many incidents of binge drinking among young people take place over spring break. For students, spring break is often a highlight of the school year. It offers a chance to take a break from rigorous academic work. During spring break, high school and college students flock to warm-weather destinations to spend time at beaches during the day and at nightclubs in the evenings. Many travel to places with a lower legal drinking age, such as Mexico. Nightclubs offer drink specials and drinking contests. According to the *Journal of American College Health*, on spring break, men consume an average of 18 drinks per day, and women consume an average of ten drinks per day.

Pediatricians Weigh In on Underage Binge Drinking

Doctors who treat young people are concerned about underage binge drinking. In April 2010, the American Academy of Pediatrics (AAP) launched its own policy on underage drinking.

The AAP policy includes 16 different recommendations about underage drinking. It calls for more screening to identify young people who are using alcohol and treatments to help those who do have an alcohol problem. The policy also recommends encouraging parents to set good examples for the children regarding alcohol, supporting the legal drinking age of 21, and continuing to stay current on research regarding alcohol and drug abuse in youth.

The group said it came out with the policy because there is such a high risk for lifetime alcohol problems in kids who start drinking at a young age. Studies have shown that people who begin drinking before age 15 are four times as likely to become dependent on alcohol in their lives. According to the NIAAA, "People who reported starting to drink before the age of 15 were four times more likely to also report meeting the criteria for alcohol dependence at some point in their lives."[3]

Binge Drinking

About spring break–related binge drinking, Dr. Katie McQueen, assistant professor of medicine at Baylor College of Medicine, said,

> It is hazardous for a number of reasons, but the biggest problems with binge drinking are the increased likelihood of trauma and impaired judgment, especially about things of a sexual nature.[4]

Many spring breakers intend to engage in casual sex, sometimes with people they do not know and without protection. McQueen also issued warnings about drinking while swimming or operating water equipment such as boats or Jet Skis—all common spring break activities. In addition to spring break, end-of-the-year proms and graduation parties are also frequently associated with heavy alcohol consumption.

Schools are aware of this. Some high schools offer school-sponsored, chaperoned spring break trips and post-prom activities. Others make efforts to offer or encourage alcohol-free activities. A University of Colorado article featured on the school's homepage offered tips for making the most of spring break. Suggested activities included getting a massage, cooking a good meal, taking a yoga class, or visiting a museum—all alternatives to the stereotypical spring break partying.

Binge Drinking

Free activities on college campuses, such as movies or game nights, aim to show young people that they can enjoy themselves without alcohol.

Chapter 7

Young people are exposed to alcohol advertising in many places.

Why Young People Drink

High school and college students binge drink for a lot of reasons—because alcohol is cheap and available, because their friends are doing it, and because movies and television shows make drinking look cool. Peer pressure is one of

Binge Drinking

the biggest reasons why young people drink. When teens see their drunk friends laughing and silly, they associate drinking with having a good time.

Young people associate drinking with a lot of positives. Many students believe that having a few glasses of beer or wine will relax them and relieve their stress. Others think they will look more mature with a glass of vodka or scotch in their hand. Sometimes people who are very shy drink alcohol to loosen up. Drinking reduces the inhibitions that prevent people from doing certain things. When shy people drink, often they become more friendly and outgoing than they normally are. A person can learn to enjoy and seek out the attention they receive while drunk.

Societal Pressure

In many television shows and movies, birthday parties, anniversaries, and weddings are celebrated with a toast of champagne or wine. Friends on television are portrayed out at bars having fun with their friends. Couples in love share romantic glasses of wine. It would seem from watching these shows and movies that everyone drinks. In reality, approximately 60 percent of adults drink alcohol.

Essential Issues

Advertising Alcohol

Research finds that kids are being exposed to a lot of alcohol ads, and those ads are making young people want to drink.

Before they graduate from high school, teens will have watched approximately 18,000 hours of television. That is more time than they will have spent in school. Every year, kids watch an average of 2,000 television commercials. Many of those commercials are for alcohol. About 20 percent of alcohol ads air during programs that people ages 12 to 20 like to watch. Kids are paying attention to these ads. One study found that 8- to 12-year-olds were able to name more brands of beer than they could name US presidents.

Advertisements make drinking seem cool and glamorous. Advertisements for alcohol feature handsome, elegant men who are surrounded by beautiful women at parties. The message to the consumer is that drinking the same alcohol as the men and women in the advertisements will ensure glamour and excitement. Alcohol companies spend a lot of money—approximately $4 billion a year—to entice people into buying their products. Alcohol ads often air during programs that young people watch, such as sports and music shows. Alcohol billboards are posted along roads where young people can easily see them. When young people see beer and other alcohol ads, they get the idea that drinking is cool and fun. Some people believe that alcohol advertisers directly market toward these younger audiences.

Binge Drinking

Drinking to Cope

Instead of drinking to fit in, some young people drink to escape. Stress, boredom, emotional pain, or dissatisfaction with circumstances might lead some young people to drink as a way to numb themselves. They might believe that alcohol is a short-term fix for dealing with a stressful situation. This can develop into a pattern of alcohol abuse that can continue into adulthood.

Price

In high school and college, students who want to buy alcohol often look for bargains. Cheaper alcohol prices entice students to buy more of it. And when a person is looking to get drunk instead of enjoying the taste of an expensive, quality bottle of alcohol, cheap liquor is not a deterrent.

Over the past five decades, the cost of alcohol has been dropping. Today, a six-pack of cheap beer costs about the same as a six-pack of soda. A 40-ounce (1,183-mL) container of malt liquor, which has a high alcohol content, can cost less than a latte at a coffee shop. To get students and young adults in the door and encourage them to buy more alcohol, bars host happy hours with half-price drinks or cheap

Essential Issues

Who Is Most Likely to Drink?

Studies have shown that certain young people are more likely to begin drinking early than others. Drinking at a young age may have to do with personality traits such as hyperactivity, aggression, disruptive behavior, depression, or anxiety. Kids who are withdrawn or rebellious are also more likely to start drinking.

Alcohol problems can be inherited—passed down from parents to their children. That is why children of alcoholics are up to ten times more likely to become alcoholics than kids whose parents do not drink heavily. It may be that parents pass these genes to their kids, or that kids see and copy their parents' drinking behaviors.

---

pitchers. Low alcohol prices make it easier to binge drink.

Availability

Alcohol is everywhere. Some communities have more liquor stores than they have restaurants or food stores. In some states, beer and wine are sold in supermarkets, just one or two aisles away from cereals and soft drinks. Gas stations and convenience stores stock plenty of alcohol. Many stores that sell alcohol are located close to homes and schools—especially colleges.

Even though alcohol is cheap and plentiful, students often do not have to make any effort at all to buy it. At college fraternity and sorority houses, pregame tailgating, and other parties, alcohol is free. Not only is it given away, but drinking it in large quantities is turned into a game. Students pour alcohol into each other's mouths through a funnel or try to bounce a quarter into a glass of beer, which they then drink.

Binge Drinking

In 2003, Yale University banned drinking games at tailgating events during the school's football game against rival Harvard University.

It might seem as though the drinking age would prevent young people from getting access to alcohol, but this is not necessarily true. More than 90 percent of high school seniors say they have had no trouble getting alcohol. They can get it from friends who are old enough to purchase it legally or find it readily available in their parents' liquor cabinets. A lot of underage drinkers who try to buy alcohol say they are successful.

Taste

Not everyone loves the taste of beer or wine, especially when they are buying cheap products. That is why liquor companies have created an entire range of drinks that are flavored to make them more appealing. Malt beverages now come in flavors such as peach, strawberry, mango, and watermelon. Lemonades and coolers contain alcohol. Vodkas and rums are also flavored. These drinks taste like candy, and they go down just as easily. Alcohol can also be made into gelatin shots, which are so sweet that it is hard to taste any of the liquor inside.

Additionally, caffeinated alcoholic beverages, which are popular with students, have been criticized for their high alcohol content. One 23.5-ounce (695-mL) can may contain as much as 12 percent alcohol, which is equivalent to approximately four beers. These alcoholic energy drinks are often fruit flavored, making them appealing to young people. The US Food and Drug Administration (FDA) has cracked down on these beverages.

Alcohol is being designed to not only taste delicious, but also to look appealing. Bars sell shots in test tubes and fish bowls. Drinks are colorful and presented in attractive glasses. Bars also sell alcoholic beverages that change the color of the drinker's tongue. All of these tactics are designed to appeal to young drinkers.

False Ideas about Drinking

Young people are naturally curious about alcohol. From what they see in

> **Myths and Facts about Drinking**
>
> Some people believe myths that justify their drinking habits. For example, an old saying goes, "Beer before liquor, never sicker. Liquor before beer, never fear." The idea is not true. It is not the type of alcohol that affects whether a person gets sick but the total amount of alcohol the person consumes.
>
> Some people believe that eating pizza or another starchy food after drinking will prevent a hangover. However, once the alcohol is inside a person's stomach, it can cause sickness or a hangover, no matter what that person eats afterward. The time to eat is before the alcohol is consumed. Having food in the stomach slows the rate at which alcohol is absorbed by the bloodstream.
>
> Another common belief is that having a cup of coffee is a good way to sober up after drinking. Although coffee can make someone who has been drinking feel more alert, it will not reverse the effects of alcohol on the body. Having a cup of coffee while drunk can actually be dangerous, giving people the false idea that they are sober enough to drive when they really are not.

Alcohol-Free Activities

Alcohol seems to be a part of college life in US culture. A student from the University of Virginia said, "Drinking is part of the social fabric in college."[1] Some schools are working to change this perception. Instead of going to fraternity and sorority parties, which are soaked with alcohol, colleges and student groups are now offering many fun, alcohol-free activity options.

For example, Temple University in Philadelphia offers its students Free Food and Fun Fridays. Every Friday night, students can watch concerts or play cards or video games for free. The school also offers alcohol-free sports and residence hall activities to ensure that students stay sober. Studies find that many students enjoy these alcohol-free activities just as much as they enjoy drinking.

the media, they believe alcohol will make them feel good. Teens may not realize that alcohol can have all sorts of unpleasant effects too, such as making them throw up and giving them a raging headache the next morning.

A lot of young people mistakenly believe that if they stick to beer, they will not be affected as much as if they drink a glass of hard liquor such as whisky or rum. That is not true. A 12-ounce (355-mL) beer contains the same amount of alcohol as a 5-ounce (148-mL) glass of wine or a 1.5-ounce (44 mL) shot of liquor. It is possible to get just as drunk or sick from beer as from hard liquor if enough of it is consumed.

Some young people say they drink as a way to relax, reduce stress, or forget about their problems. What they may not realize is that alcohol can create many problems of its own.

Binge Drinking

Colorful drinks and gelatin shots appeal to young people.

Chapter 8

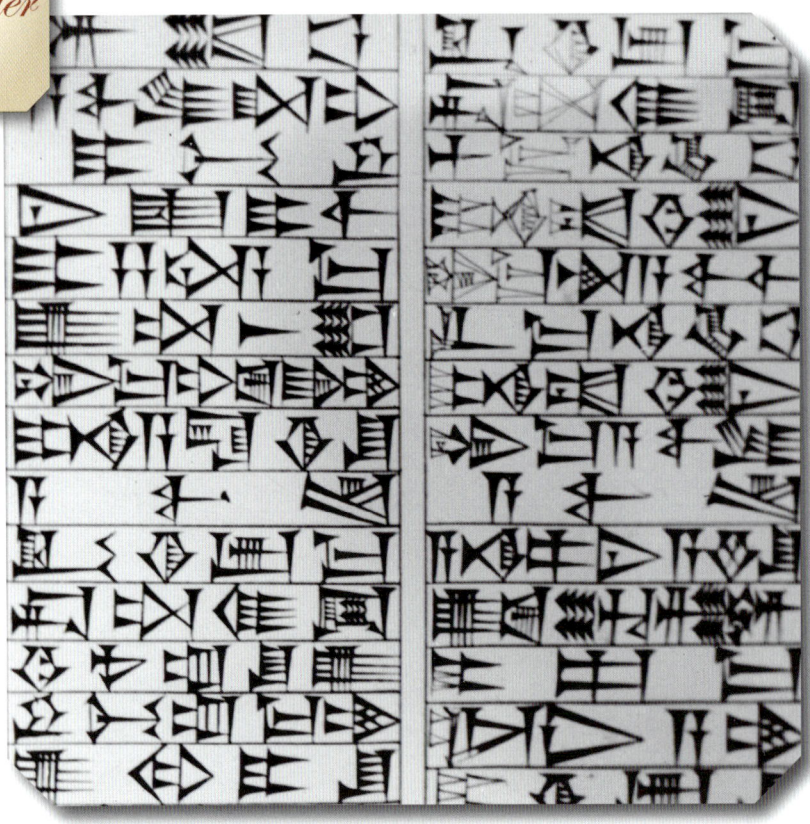

A portion of the ancient Code of Hammurabi

Laws to Stop Binge Drinking

Throughout history, governments have enacted laws to make it harder for people to consume large amounts of alcohol. Other laws have attempted to make it more difficult for people under the drinking age to acquire alcohol. Some of these laws have been successful, but some have proven otherwise.

Early Efforts to Curb Binge Drinking

One early written law was the Code of Hammurabi, written by King Hammurabi of Mesopotamia around 1750 BCE. The code did not punish drunkenness. However, it did name a strict punishment for tavern owners who modified drinks to get their patrons drunk. They were to be drowned.

It was not until the middle of the sixteenth century that drunkenness was first mentioned as a crime in England. To combat the problem, in 1603, England's Parliament passed an act imposing a penalty of ten shillings on any inn owner who allowed his patrons to become drunk. This was followed by a 1606 act that penalized the drinker with a fine of five shillings or, if they could not pay, six hours in the stocks—a form of public humiliation.

Many early governments had laws against the production of alcoholic beverages. However, these laws often did not last long. Governments knew that where there was wine and beer, there was also money to be made in taxes. In the 1600s, England's government used taxes to control the production

Essential Issues

Anti-Saloon League

The Anti-Saloon League, founded in 1893, was one of a few organizations lobbying the US government for prohibition in the early 1900s. Like many other pro-prohibition groups, the Anti-Saloon League was a religious organization. It used the power of churches and their members to push for anti-drinking laws. The group called itself "the united Church Militant engaged in the overthrow of the liquor traffic" and said its aim was "not to uplift the individual drunkard, but to remove the cause of his degradation."[1]

The Anti-Saloon League set up its own publishing company, which printed billions of pages of propaganda about alcohol and its ill effects. As part of this effort, the league mocked people and cultures that produced or used alcohol, including Germans, Jews, Irish, and Italians.

of distilled spirits—and to make a little extra money for itself. In 1862, the US Congress imposed a tax on liquor (as well as on other luxury items) to help fund the Civil War. To avoid paying taxes, many people began making their own liquor called moonshine. Moonshine became even more popular once the distribution of alcohol was abolished entirely during Prohibition.

Prohibition

In the 1800s, religious groups and other organizations began calling for temperance, or moderation in drinking. Groups such as the Anti-Saloon League and the Woman's Christian Temperance Union started pushing hard for local prohibition laws. They felt that drinking alcohol was bad for people and US society, and they wanted to wipe it out completely.

In 1919, they scored a big victory. On January 16, the Eighteenth

Binge Drinking

Prohibition agents poured out seized alcohol into the Elizabeth River in Virginia in 1922.

Amendment to the US Constitution was ratified, making the production and sale of alcohol illegal. A year later, Prohibition went into effect, prohibiting the sale or production of alcohol in the United States. Yet the alcohol trade did not stop—instead, it went underground. Saloons and bars disguised themselves as other businesses. These speakeasies, as they were called, were illegal, but they thrived. Moonshiners who made their own liquor thrived too. The alcohol industry remained underground until 1933, when Prohibition was finally repealed with the passage of the Twenty-First Amendment. Since the repeal of the Prohibition laws, many have speculated about the success of the amendment to prohibit alcohol sale and distribution in the United States. Some believe that under Prohibition, moderate drinkers became binge drinkers instead.

After Prohibition, the government tried to refine its laws against drunkenness and alcohol. Alcohol abuse was no longer seen as a criminal offense. Instead of locking people up to punish them for drinking, efforts were made to get them treated for their alcohol-related problems. Alcohol laws began shifting in the latter part of the twentieth century to discourage underage drinking and dangerous acts, such as driving, done under the influence of alcohol.

Limiting Alcohol Sales

Many states have attempted to curb excessive and underage drinking by placing limitations on alcohol sales, making alcohol harder for young people to get. One way to do this is to limit the places where alcohol can be sold. In some states, alcohol can only be purchased in liquor stores—not in convenience stores or supermarkets. People who work in alcohol stores are trained to check the identification of each patron attempting to purchase alcohol. They have to make sure alcohol purchasers are of legal age.

Stores that sell alcohol may not be allowed within a certain distance of schools or homes. Some public places, such as parks, beaches, and festivals, limit or do not allow the sale of alcohol. In many states, it is illegal to buy alcohol on the Internet and ship it to a home address. This law is designed to prevent underage drinkers from ordering alcohol online.

Drunk Driving Laws

Drunk driving laws are not intended to stop people from drinking, but instead, to prevent them from getting behind the wheel of a car after they have been drinking. Every state has laws that make it illegal to drive with a BAC of .08 percent or higher.

People who break these laws by driving while over the illegal limit can have their driver's license suspended for between three months and a year. In more than half of the states, people who drive while drunk can have their car taken away. Some people might be sentenced to install an ignition interlock in their vehicles. The device includes a Breathalyzer that prohibits the car from starting if the driver's BAC is over the illegal limit. Additionally, insurance rates can skyrocket for drivers arrested or convicted of drunk driving.

Raising the Drinking Age

The legal drinking age was created as a way to prevent young people from having access to alcohol. After Prohibition, the drinking age in most states was 21—the same age at which a person could vote. In 1971, the Twenty-Sixth Amendment to the US Constitution lowered the national voting age to 18. Within the next few years, 29 states also lowered their drinking age to 18, 19, or 20.

Then a few studies found that the number of car accidents had increased after the drinking age was lowered. Advocacy groups such as Mothers Against Drunk Driving (MADD) began lobbying the government to increase the drinking age back to 21. On April 14, 1982, President Ronald Reagan established the Presidential Commission on Drunk Driving to reduce the number of alcohol-related deaths. The commission made dozens of recommendations, including that states raise their drinking age, increase penalties for drunk drivers, and launch youth alcohol education programs.

Facing pressure from MADD and other groups like it, on July 17, 1984, President Reagan signed the National Minimum Drinking Age Act. This act officially raised the drinking age to 21 throughout the country. States that did not increase their drinking age would lose part of their federal transportation funds.

Mothers Against Drunk Driving

On a spring day in 1980, Candy Lightner received the news every parent dreads. Her 13-year-old daughter Cari had been struck and killed by a drunk driver while walking to a church carnival. At the time, there were almost no laws prohibiting drinking and driving. Lightner decided to turn her grief into a cause: to stop drunk driving.

She started an organization, which she called Mothers Against Drunk Driving (MADD). At first, she ran MADD out of Cari's bedroom. Then the donations began pouring in. Many of them came from other mothers who had experienced the same kind of loss. MADD chapters popped up around the country. By 1982, MADD had 100 chapters. In 1984, the number had increased to 330 chapters in 47 states.

MADD fought hard to get new driving under the influence (DUI) laws passed. In 1982, the group pressed President Reagan to form the Presidential Commission on Drunk Driving. By 1983, 129 new drunk driving laws had been passed. In July 1984, MADD helped push the Uniform Drinking Age Act into law. In 2000, the group scored another victory when the illegal BAC driving limit was lowered to .08. MADD says that since it was launched, its efforts have saved more than 300,000 lives.

Candy Lightner pinned a MADD button on President Ronald Reagan after he signed the National Minimum Drinking Age Act in 1984.

Studies done after the act went into effect found that raising the minimum drinking age did reduce the number of young drinkers. It also reduced the number of injuries and deaths in alcohol-related

Binge Drinking

accidents. The National Highway Transportation Safety Administration (NHTSA) estimates that raising the legal drinking age to 21 saves between 700 and 1,000 lives each year. However, safer cars and stricter drunk driving laws may also have had an impact on accident-related deaths.

Some experts argue that raising the minimum drinking age actually did not do much to stop underage drinking. They say that, because the laws are not well enforced, many young people still have easy access to alcohol and the drinking is now driven underground, making enforcement even more difficult. Additionally, the fear of being caught might prevent underage drinkers from calling 911 if someone passes out and needs medical attention, and this could have deadly consequences. Others believe stopping binge drinking requires more than just assessing the drinking age. In 2008, an editorial in the *New York Times* stated,

Loopholes in the Minimum Drinking Age

The national legal drinking age in the United States is 21. Certain states allow people who are under age 21 to sell alcohol in a bar or liquor store, even though they are not legally old enough to drink it. Even though selling alcohol to minors is illegal in all states, some states do not specifically prohibit young people from consuming alcohol.

There are exceptions for certain situations. Young people can legally have alcohol as part of religious ceremonies, such as taking communion wine in church, or for medical reasons. They also can drink alcohol in their own homes with their parents.

Choose Responsibility

Groups such as MADD argue that having a higher drinking age saves lives. Not everyone agrees, however. In 2008, a group of college presidents, including the presidents of Duke and Dartmouth Universities, wrote a petition pushing for public debate over the drinking age. John McCardle, former president of Middlebury College in Vermont, started a whole movement around this idea. He called it "Choose Responsibility."

This movement seeks to lower the drinking age to 18—the same age at which young people are allowed to vote and serve in the military. The idea behind lowering the drinking age is that taking away the forbidden thrill of drinking will make drinking less appealing. McCardle believes that increasing education and awareness about the issues and side effects involved with alcohol consumption will make young people drink more responsibly.

"The 21-year-old floor [drinking age] is not the problem. It is the culture of drinking at school."[2] The debate over the legal drinking age continues with everyone from law enforcement, college staff, and parents weighing in.

Binge Drinking

In England, the legal age to purchase alcohol is 18. Even though the age is lower than in the United States, binge drinking remains a problem.

Chapter 9

A woman passes a window display in London, England, that is part of an advertising campaign against binge drinking.

Other Efforts to Prevent Binge Drinking

Not all efforts to reduce binge drinking have started with the government. Many states, local communities, and schools have also launched their own efforts to prevent both binge and underage drinking. In some cases, partnerships exist between law enforcement and local citizens with the intent to raise awareness about alcohol abuse and cut down on incidents of binge drinking.

Reducing Alcohol Advertising

Research has found that watching alcohol advertisements does not necessarily make people want to drink alcohol—it just makes them prefer one alcohol brand over another. Still, exposure to alcohol ads does give young people a more positive feeling about drinking. It also makes them more likely to start drinking while they are still underage.

Reducing the number of ads in programs that young people watch is one way to lower their exposure to alcohol. Another way is to produce ads that promote drinking safety. In the 1980s, a series of ads promoted the use of a "designated driver." A designated driver is one person

Anti-Binge Drinking Ads

Advertising is a very effective way to get out the message about the negative effects of binge drinking to a lot of young people at once. One ad from England shows a girl tearing her clothes, smearing her makeup, and throwing up as she gets ready for a night out. The tagline reads, "You wouldn't start a night like this, so why end it that way?"[1] An ad from Australia depicts another of the possible hazards of binge drinking—a girl being sexually assaulted by several young men while she is passed out drunk at a party. These ads provide sobering reminders about the dangers of binge drinking.

who stays sober to drive his or her drunken friends home after a night of drinking. Thanks to this campaign, many people today are familiar with the idea of designated drivers, and many people have a designated driver whenever they plan to drink.

State Regulations

Federal and state laws preventing underage drinking exist, but they are not well enforced. Most states do not have the funding to check every single liquor store and bar and make sure they do not sell alcohol to minors. Police are not able to pull over every single driver to check whether he or she is drunk.

Yet states have put policies in place that are effective. Some states do not allow people to drink from open alcohol containers in public. Other states do not allow billboards and other types of alcohol advertising. People who buy beer in kegs may have to register the kegs with their name and personal information and prove that they are over 21. Some states encourage random checkpoints on roads to look for impaired drivers. Studies have found that college students are less likely to drink in states that have strict alcohol control policies.

Community Programs

Many local communities have taken alcohol prevention efforts into their own hands to reduce underage drinking and alcohol-related injuries. Part of this effort involves teaching sales clerks at liquor stores how to spot fake or borrowed IDs used by young people to purchase alcohol. Lending, using, or making a false ID is illegal, and penalties could include heavy fines or jail time. Additionally, the criminal offense can appear on a young person's permanent record, which could negatively affect future job prospects or college admissions.

Other efforts are designed to make drinking a less acceptable activity in the community. Some community programs work with families and schools to give kids the anti-drinking message in every area of their lives. For example, Communities That Care is a program

Project Northland

Project Northland was a community-wide effort sponsored by the NIAAA. Beginning in the early 1990s, it involved 24 school districts and 28 nearby communities in Minnesota. Project Northland targeted every aspect of kids' lives, including their parents, siblings, friends, teachers, coaches, religious leaders, schools, peers, local business owners, and government leaders. Students learned about the dangers of alcohol use and how to resist peer pressure. Parents also learned strategies to prevent their kids from drinking.

The program started in sixth grade. It followed more than 2,300 students all the way through high school. After three years, the results were tallied. Project Northland cut the number of students who drank by about a third. It showed how a community-wide anti-drinking effort could have a big effect on the number of kids drinking.

Essential Issues

Youth to Youth is a drug prevention program for middle and high school students. Youth to Youth protesters rallied in New Hampshire in 2008.

of the US Government's Substance and Mental Health Services Administration. It was created to reduce problems such as school dropout, teen pregnancy, and alcohol abuse among young people. Many communities around the country are following this program. These communities work closely with schools and families to foster healthy, productive

Binge Drinking

kids and support more positive behaviors among young people.

School Programs and Policies

As early as elementary school, kids are introduced to anti-drinking programs. One such program is Drug Abuse Resistance Education (D.A.R.E.). In the D.A.R.E. program, local law enforcement officers visit schools to teach students about drugs, alcohol, and violence. Students learn about the dangers of drugs and alcohol and how to resist peer pressure. In the United States, three-fourths of school districts have implemented a D.A.R.E. program. The program also has spread to more than 40 countries worldwide. Despite its popularity, research shows that the D.A.R.E. program may not be effective at preventing drug abuse. Some criticize its lack of flexibility. Other programs emphasize parental involvement, including Families and Schools Together and Project ALERT.

Alcohol education efforts are important in colleges too. Nearly all colleges have some form of alcohol education—especially for high-risk students such as freshmen, fraternity and sorority members, and athletes. These programs teach

Essential Issues

students how to drink responsibly. At the University of Colorado, for example, all freshmen are required to take an alcohol awareness course. However, not all of these programs are effective. Author Barrett Seaman, who studied binge drinking and campus life, wrote, "When administrations try to crack down, they drive drinking underground, like Prohibition."[2]

One-third of colleges ban all alcohol use on campus—even among students who are age 21 and over. Some religious colleges, especially Christian evangelical schools, require students to sign a covenant, or agreement, promising that they will abstain from certain activities such as drinking and drug use during their time at the school. Many colleges also arrange alcohol-free recreational activities such as movie nights and dances. They may offer alcohol-free residences and closely monitor

Safe Homes

Parents are influential in a teen's life. To prevent their kids from drinking, many parents around the country are taking the Safe Homes Pledge. Parents who take this pledge promise to:
- Supervise all parties in their homes
- Not serve alcohol to anyone under age 21
- Not allow any young person to have or use tobacco, alcohol, or drugs on their home or property
- Have their name and phone number published in school handouts or newspapers to let other parents know they have signed the Safe Homes Pledge

fraternities and sororities to make sure drinking does not get out of hand and that any illegal drinking is punished. Colleges and universities are required to print annual statistics on arrests and discipline for alcohol-related incidents.

Studies have found that alcohol-prevention efforts on campus can reduce heavy drinking by as much as 35 percent. These programs can also reduce alcohol-related injuries by more than a third. In contrast, some schools do not attempt to prevent alcohol use entirely, but instead use a harm-reduction approach. This approach acknowledges that a society will never be entirely drug and alcohol free and seeks to implement practical solutions to the harms caused by drug abuse.

Changing Perceptions about Drinking

Because so many positive messages about alcohol reach young people, experts say it is important for students to also see the downsides of drinking. They need to see that alcohol can lead to hangovers and blackouts and the kinds of long-term health problems that can ruin lives. For example, many countries have launched anti-drinking campaigns aimed at young people. In the United States, some ads do target binge drinking. However, most prevention efforts in the country are aimed at illegal drugs or tobacco. Alcohol use is more widespread and kills more young people than drugs or cigarettes.

Alcohol Prices and Binge Drinking

Studies have found that fewer young people drink when alcohol prices are high. Less drinking means fewer alcohol-related problems, so some people have proposed raising alcohol prices as a quick fix to this issue. Yet this might not be as simple as it seems.

Some experts argue that increasing the price of alcohol would only unfairly punish the many adults who drink responsibly. Additionally, a large number of binge drinkers are adults who can afford to buy expensive alcohol, so raised prices would not fix the problem. Instead,

A Community Program That Worked

In 1988, the state of Massachusetts launched the Massachusetts Saving Lives Program to combat drunk driving. The program involved city officials and private citizens. It introduced drunk driving checkpoints, drunk driving awareness days, high school and college drinking prevention programs, alcohol-free prom nights, and other programs.

After five years, fatal crashes—especially those involving drivers ages 15 to 25—dropped by 42 percent. The number of 16- to 19-year-olds who reported drinking after driving also dropped.

some focus on making alcohol less accessible to young people.

Making Alcohol Harder to Get

It is very difficult to limit alcohol sales to people who are over 21, but there are laws against underage drinking. They just need to be better enforced. One way to enforce underage drinking laws is to make sure bars and stores that sell alcohol are staffed with trained professionals who know how to check IDs. Another way to discourage alcohol use in minors is to have adults oversee places where kids hang out, and keep a closer watch on kids who are at risk for binge drinking.

However, not all underage drinkers have to go to the store to acquire alcohol. Many can find it in their homes and can drink without their parents even knowing it. In some extreme cases when alcohol is not available, young people and alcoholics have turned to dangerous alternatives. To get drunk, they might consume inexpensive types of alcohol, such as rubbing alcohol, which is significantly more toxic to the body.

For these reasons, parents need to be closely involved, especially as they help inform their

Essential Issues

children's perceptions of alcohol. Parents can model responsible drinking, but there are other things they can do too. Jane Curtis is the director of the Alcohol and Other Drugs Program at the University of Colorado. She urges parents to engage in honest discussions with their children regarding the dangers of alcohol abuse. "We know that students are engaging and talking with parents more," she said in 2009.[3] Curtis emphasizes that it is important for parents to have these conversations about alcohol before their children go to college.

Alcoholics Anonymous

There are many programs available to help people who have a drinking problem. One of the most famous of these programs is Alcoholics Anonymous (AA). AA was started in 1935 by two men who had experienced problems with alcohol throughout their lives. Since then, it has spread to countless communities and countries worldwide.

The AA method involves regular meetings for alcoholics who offer each other accountability and encouragement. The only requirement for attending a meeting is a person's wish to become sober. Because other group members have had problems with alcohol, the groups are a safe, comfortable place where a person can receive empathetic help from people experiencing the same types of struggles.

AA uses a 12-step program to help problem drinkers get sober and stay that way. The first of these steps requires the person to recognize that he or she has an alcohol problem. The method also emphasizes taking one day at a time. Although AA mentions reliance on God, or a higher power, in its program, it stresses that it is not a religious organization, and people of all faiths—even atheists or agnostics—are welcome to join.

Binge Drinking

How Teens Can Get Help

Because statistics show that alcohol abuse is common among teens, the American Academy of Pediatrics says pediatricians need to get involved by asking their patients whether they drink. They can also ask parents whether their children drink alcohol, and if so, how much. However, not all doctors take the time to talk to their patients about alcohol. Many young people binge drink without anyone knowing about it, and they never get the treatment they need.

Young people who think they or their friends have a problem with alcohol should get help right away. They should talk to a parent, school counselor, clergy member, or another trusted adult. Teenagers who have an alcohol problem can get help through their school counselor or family doctor, or by attending meetings of an alcohol-counseling program such as Alcoholics Anonymous. Taking the first step and getting help could save a life.

In encouraging teens to make smart choices regarding alcohol, doctors and activists encourage teens to consider their growing bodies and the importance of taking care of themselves. The choices young people make today influence the people they will become. Dr. Jay Geidd, an expert in brain

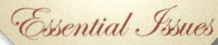

imaging at the National Institutes of Health, stated, "Teens, through their choices and actions, have the power to direct the development of their own brains."4

Binge Drinking

In March 2010, Maryland high school students listened to a presentation about a death caused by drunk driving.

Essential Issues

Timeline

2000 BCE
The Sumerian civilization uses beer and wine as medical treatments.

1750 BCE
The Code of Hammurabi establishes the penalty of death by drowning for tavern owners who try to get their patrons drunk.

circa 400 BCE
Hippocrates, the father of Western medicine, promotes the use of wine to treat nearly every ailment.

1689
The British Parliament opens up distillation to a wider number of businesses, prompting the Gin Epidemic.

1751
The Tippling Act is passed in England, imposing restrictions on gin sales.

early 1800s
The temperance movement gains momentum in the United States.

Binge Drinking

1600s
Gin is invented, but only a small number of British companies are allowed to operate distilleries.

1603
England's Parliament passes an act imposing a penalty of ten shillings on any inn owner who allows his patrons to become drunk.

1606
England's Parliament passes an act penalizing public drunkenness with a fine of five shillings or six hours in the stocks.

1861–1865
During the American Civil War, beer is called "liquid bread" because it provides nutrients lacking in soldiers' diets.

1919
The Eighteenth Amendment to the Constitution, otherwise known as Prohibition, is ratified on January 16. It goes into effect the next year.

1933
The Twenty-First Amendment to the Constitution is ratified on December 5, repealing Prohibition.

Timeline

1930s

Researcher E. Morton Jellinek of Yale University begins studying problem drinking.

1945

The movie *The Lost Weekend* is released, showing movie viewers the horrors of binge drinking.

1952

Jellinek describes alcoholism as a disease, which begins changing the public's opinion about drinking.

1994

Social psychologist Henry Wechsler defines binge drinking as five or more drinks for men and four or more drinks for women.

1997

Eighteen-year-old Scott Krueger attends a fraternity event and consumes 15 shots of alcohol in an hour. He later dies from alcohol poisoning.

2004

In September, 19-year old Samantha Spady is found dead in a fraternity house after binge drinking.

Binge Drinking

1971

The national voting age is lowered to 18. Within the next few years, 29 states lower their drinking age to 18, 19, or 20.

1982

On April 14, President Ronald Reagan establishes the Presidential Commission on Drunk Driving.

1984

On July 17, Reagan signs the National Minimum Drinking Age Act, raising the national drinking age to 21.

2004

Lynn Gordon Bailey Jr., an 18-year-old college student, dies from binge drinking.

2009

On June 22, 16-year-old Scott Eugene Roberts attends a party and consumes 24 alcohol shots. He is pronounced dead the next morning.

2010

In April, the American Academy of Pediatrics launches its own policy on underage drinking.

Essential Issues

Essential Facts

At Issue

❖ In the past, people who drank heavily were seen as weak or unable to control themselves. Today, binge drinking and alcoholism are considered health problems that need to be treated.

❖ The definition of binge drinking most researchers use is five or more drinks in one sitting for men and four or more drinks in one sitting for women.

❖ Binge drinking is a concern to health officials because it puts people at greater risk for health problems and injuries.

❖ The rate of binge drinking is highest among the 15–24 age group, but many kids start drinking alcohol as early as middle school. By age 13, about one-third of kids say they have started drinking.

❖ High school and college students binge drink in part because of peer pressure, low alcohol prices, and positive messages about alcohol from movies and television shows.

❖ Government, school, and community programs have tried to prevent binge drinking by educating kids about the perils of alcohol and reducing young people's access to alcohol.

Critical Dates

1952
Researcher E. Morton Jellinek of Yale University began changing public opinion about alcohol abuse when he described it as a disease. Up until this time, society viewed drunks as weak and unable to control themselves. Jellinek identified alcoholism as a medical condition.

Binge Drinking

1994
Harvard University social psychologist Henry Wechsler issued a definition of binge drinking that is used by many organizations today. Under his definition, binge drinking is five or more drinks in one sitting for men and four or more drinks in one sitting for women. However, some groups refuse to use this definition, claiming it does not take into account other important factors, such as the amount of time over which the drinks are consumed.

2010
In April, the American Academy of Pediatrics launched its own policy on underage drinking. The policy included recommendations, including encouraging physicians to screen young people who are using alcohol and treat those who do have an alcohol problem.

Quotes

"Binge drinking is associated with over half of the 79 thousand alcohol-attributable deaths in the United States each year."
—*Dr. Robert Brewer, alcohol program leader for the National Center for Chronic Disease Prevention and Health Promotion at the CDC*

"Alcohol remains the most heavily abused substance by America's youth. We can no longer ignore what alcohol is doing to our children. . . . Underage drinking is everybody's problem—and its solution is everyone's responsibility." —*Former acting surgeon general Kenneth P. Moritsugu*

Glossary

alcoholic
Someone who drinks excessively on a regular basis and who is physically addicted to alcohol.

bender
A drinking spree that can last for several days.

Breathalyzer
A piece of equipment that measures the amount of alcohol in the breath to determine a person's BAC.

cirrhosis
A disease often caused by drinking too much alcohol, leading to damage and scarring of the liver.

dehydration
Losing too much water from the body.

depressant
A substance, such as alcohol, that slows down the body's functions.

distillation
A process used to make alcoholic beverages such as whiskey by heating and purification.

fermentation
The process by which yeast breaks down sugar to produce carbon dioxide and alcohol. Fermentation is used to make alcoholic beverages such as beer and wine.

hallucination
A sensory experience of something that does not exist outside the mind.

intoxication
> A state of excitement, euphoria, or loss of control that occurs after drinking alcohol.

metabolism
> The chemical processes in the body by which substances are broken down to release energy.

moonshine
> Alcohol that is distilled illegally by people who do not have a license to produce it.

pancreas
> The organ that makes digestive enzymes and the hormone insulin.

Prohibition
> The period from 1920 to 1933 in which alcohol was illegal to produce or sell in the United States.

seizures
> Tremors and other symptoms that occur due to abnormal electric activity in the brain.

stroke
> An interruption in the brain's blood supply.

temperance
> Moderation or avoidance of alcohol.

vandalism
> The intentional damaging of another person's property.

Additional Resources

Selected Bibliography

"Alcohol and Public Health Fact Sheets: Binge Drinking." *Centers for Disease Control and Prevention*. N.p., n.d. Web.

Berridge, Virginia, Rachel Herring, and Betsy Thom. "Binge Drinking: A Confused Concept and Its Contemporary History." *Social History of Medicine*. 22 Dec. 2009: 597–607. *Oxford Journals*. Oxford UP, n.d. Web.

"Binge Drinking on College Campuses." *Center for Science in the Public Interest*. N.p., n.d. Web.

Miller, Jacqueline W., Timothy S. Naimi, Robert D. Brewer, and Sherry Everett Jones. "Binge Drinking and Associated Health Risk Behaviors Among High School Students." *Pediatrics*. 1 Jan. 2007: 76–85. *Pediatrics*. American Academy of Pediatrics, 2 Jan. 2007. Web.

Further Readings

Aretha, David. *On the Rocks: Teens and Alcohol*. New York: Franklin Watts, 2007. Print.

Friedman, Lauri S., ed. *Alcohol*. Farmington Hills, MI: Greenhaven, 2010. Print.

Volkmann, Chris. *From Binge to Blackout: A Mother and Son Struggle with Teen Drinking*. New York: New American Library, 2006. Print.

Web Links

To learn more about binge drinking, visit ABDO Publishing Company online at **www.abdopublishing.com**. Web sites about binge drinking are featured on our Book Links page. These links are routinely monitored and updated to provide the most current information available.

For More Information

For more information on this subject, contact or visit the following organizations:

The Century Council
2345 Crystal Drive, Suite 910, Arlington, VA 22202
202-637-0077
www.centurycouncil.org
This group, which was founded in 1991 by distillers, supports programs to prevent underage drinking. The group sponsors a Web site, alcohol101plus.org, aimed specifically at helping college students make responsible choices about alcohol.

National Institute on Alcohol Abuse and Alcoholism (NIAAA)
5635 Fishers Lane, MSC 9304, Bethesda, MD 20892-9304
301-443-3860
www.niaaa.nih.gov/Pages/default.aspx
The NIAAA conducts research on alcohol prevention and treatment and shares the results of that research with the public.

Students Against Destructive Decisions (SADD)
255 Main Street, Marlborough, MA 01752
1-877-SADD-INC
www.sadd.org
Formerly Students Against Drunk Driving, this peer-to-peer organization seeks to give students tools and information to make responsible decisions.

Source Notes

Chapter 1. A Life Lost
1. "Surgeon General's Call to Action to Prevent and Reduce Underage Drinking." *U.S. Department of Health and Human Services*. U.S. Department of Health and Human Services, 2007. Web. 1 Jan 2011.

Chapter 2. The History of Binge Drinking
None.

Chapter 3. Is Binge Drinking on the Rise?
None.

Chapter 4. What Happens When People Binge Drink
None.

Chapter 5. How Binge Drinking Affects Lives
1. "CDC Features: Binge Drinking." *Centers for Disease Control and Prevention*. N.p., 14 Apr. 2010. Web. 1 Jan 2011.
2. Jason Robertson. "Flatwater Study Finds Alcohol Boosts Drowning Risk." *American Whitewater*. American Whitewater, 19 Dec. 2001. Web. 24 Mar. 2011.

Chapter 6. Binge Drinking and Young People
    1. "Underage Drinking." *PreventUnderageDrinkingNM.org*. N.p., Mar. 2008. Web. 24 Mar. 2011.
    2. Lynne Peeples. "Binge drinking, pot may harm teen brains." *CNNHealth*. Cable News Network, 19 Oct. 2010. Web. 26 Apr. 2011.
    3. "Underage Drinking: Why Do Adolescents Drink, What Are the Risks, and How Can Underage Drinking Be Prevented?" *National Institute on Alcohol Abuse and Alcoholism*. National Institute on Alcohol Abuse and Alcoholism, Jan. 2006. Web. 26 Apr. 2010.
    4. Dana Benson. "Binge drinking: Be aware of dangers during spring break." *Baylor College of Medicine*. Baylor College of Medicine, 19 Mar. 2008. Web. 24 Mar. 2011.

Chapter 7. Why Young People Drink
    1. John H. Tucker. "Fighting Binge Drinking on Campus? It Takes a Village." *Newsweek Education*. Newsweek, Inc., 1 Dec. 2010. Web. 24 Mar. 2011.

Source Notes Continued

Chapter 8. Laws to Stop Binge Drinking

1. William Hamilton Anderson. *The Church in Action Against the Saloon*. Westerville, OH: American Issue Publishing Co., 1910. *Google Books*. Web. 24 Mar. 2011.

2. "Colleges and Binge Drinking." *The New York Times*. The New York Times Company, 16 Sept. 2008. Web. 24 Mar. 2011.

Chapter 9. Other Efforts to Prevent Binge Drinking

1. "Binge-drinking adverts launched." *BBC*. BBC, 17 June 2008. Web. 24 Mar. 2011.

2. John H. Tucker. "Fighting Binge Drinking on Campus? It Takes a Village." *Newsweek Education*. Newsweek, Inc., 1 Dec. 2010. Web. 24 Mar. 2011.

3. Kimberly Crater. "Battling Binge Drinking at the University of Colorado." *Addictioninfo.org*. Myaddiction.com, 29 Apr. 2009. Web. 24 Mar. 2011.

4. Underage Drinking." *PreventUnderageDrinkingNM.org*. N.p., Mar. 2008. Web. 24 Mar. 2011.

Index

alcohol
   advertising, 62, 83, 84
   availability, 60, 64–66, 91
   drinking games, 7, 64
   health benefits, 23
   myths and facts, 67
   prices, 19, 60, 63–64, 90–91
   taste, 63, 66–67
alcohol content, 9, 63, 66
Alcohol Drug Abuse Resource Center, 29
alcohol poisoning, 7, 37, 38
Alcoholics Anonymous, 92, 93
alcoholism, 7, 22, 23, 35, 40, 50, 55, 64, 91, 92
American Academy of Pediatrics, 56, 93
Anti-Saloon League, 72

Babylonians, 17
Bailey, Lynn Gordon, Jr., 12
Baltz, Leslie, 47
benders, 22, 24
binge drinking
   definition, 7–10
   and geography, 32
   history, 16–24
   physical effects of, 34–40
   problems with the definition, 10–12
blood alcohol content, 7, 10, 11–12, 35, 43, 44, 46, 75, 76, 77
Breathalyzers, 44, 76

cardiopulmonary resuscitation, 7
Centers for Disease Control and Prevention, US, 9–10, 11, 29, 49
cirrhosis, 37–38, 55
Civil War, 23, 72
Code of Hammurabi, 71
Communities That Care, 85
community programs, 85–87, 90
Congress, US, 72
consequences of binge drinking
   blackouts, 43, 89
   drowning, 48, 49
   drunk driving, 9, 38–39, 43, 44, 45–46, 67, 74, 75–76, 77, 79, 84, 90
   injuries, 9, 44, 47–49, 78, 85, 89
   rape and sexual assault, 47, 83
   unsafe sex, 43, 44, 57
   vandalism, 9, 43, 49
   violence, 35, 46–47
covenants, 88
Curtis, Jane, 92

Department of Justice, US, 31
designated drivers, 83–84
drinking age, 27, 56, 65, 76–80
Drug Abuse Resistance Education, 87
drunk driving laws, 75–76, 77, 79

Index Continued

Egyptians, 17
Eighteenth Amendment, 72–73
enforcing alcohol laws, 79, 84, 91

Families and Schools Together, 87
fermentation, 17
field sobriety tests, 44
Food and Drug Administration, US, 67
Foss, Robert D., 49
fraternities, 12, 28, 38, 64, 68, 87, 89

Geidd, Jay, 93
Gin Epidemic, 19

Harvard School of Public Health, 28
Hippocrates, 21

Industrial Revolution, 20
Inter-Association Task Force on Alcohol and Other Substance Abuse Issues, 12

Jellinek, E. Morton, 23
Journal of American College Health, 57

King Hammurabi, 71
Krueger, Scott, 38

Lightner, Candy, 77
Lost Weekend, The, 22–23

Mary, Queen of Scots, 18
Massachusetts Saving Lives Program, 90
McCardle, John, 80
McQueen, Katie, 57
metabolism, 8, 10, 35
Middle Ages, 18, 19
moonshine, 72, 74
Moritsugu, Kenneth P., 14
Mothers Against Drunk Driving, 76, 77, 80

National Highway Transportation Safety Administration, 79
National Institute on Alcohol Abuse and Alcoholism, 12, 56, 85
National Institute on Drug Abuse, 10
National Institutes of Health, 94
National Minimum Drinking Age Act, 77
Nelson, Toben F., 29

peer pressure, 28, 60, 85, 87
Presidential Commission on Drunk Driving, 76, 77
Prohibition Era, 22, 72–74, 76, 88
Project ALERT, 87
Project Northland, 85
prom, 57, 90
Public Health College Alcohol Study, 8

Reagan, Ronald, 76, 77
Roberts, Scott Eugene, 6–7, 12

Safe Homes Pledge, 88
Seaman, Barrett, 88
sororities, 28, 64, 68, 87, 89
Spady, Samantha, 12
spring break, 56–58
Substance and Mental Health Services Administration, 86
Sumerian civilization, 17
Surgeon General, US, 9, 14

temperance movement, 21, 72
Third National Health and Nutrition Survey, 54
Thoma, Robert J., 53
Tippling Act, 19
Tudors, 18
Twenty-First Amendment, 74
Twenty-Sixth Amendment, 76

Uniform Drinking Age Act, 77

Wechsler, Henry, 8–9, 10, 11, 12, 24, 29
Wernicke-Korsakoff syndrome, 40
White, Aaron, 53
Woman's Christian Temperance Union, 72

Yale University, 23

About the Author

Stephanie Watson is an award-winning freelance writer based in Atlanta, Georgia. After working as a television on-air promotion writer and producer, she launched a successful career writing for books, magazines, and the Internet. She has written or contributed to more than two dozen books.

Photo Credits

Garry Wade/Getty Images, cover, 3; Alejandro Rivera/iStockphoto, 6; Bill Hafer/AP Images, 13, 98 (bottom); Kevin Buey/AP Images, 15; North Wind Picture Archives, 16, 97 (top); Hulton Archive/Getty Images, 21; Paramount Pictures/Getty Images, 25, 98 (top); Neal Hamberg/AP Images, 26; Morry Gash/AP Images, 30; Keith Muccilli/AP Images, 33; Forest Woodward/iStockphoto, 34; Shutterstock Images, 39; Jeff Geissler/AP Images, 41; Marion R Walding/AP Images, 42; Jim Mone/AP Images, 45; John Kuntz/The Plain Dealer/AP Images, 48; Francois Nascimbeni/AFP/Getty Images, 51; AP Images, 52, 78, 99; Rich Legg/iStockphoto, 59; Mario Tama/Getty Images, 60; Abigail Reider/AP Images, 65; iStockphoto, 69; Kean Collection/Getty Images, 70, 96; Charles S. Borjes/Virginian-Pilot/AP Images, 73, 97 (bottom); Gabriele Stabile/Getty Images, 81; Cate Gillon/Getty Images, 82; Jim Cole/AP Images, 86; The Washington Post/Getty Images, 95